AGAINST

ALL

ODDS

CEDRIC WESTBROOK

NEWMAN SPRINGS PUBLISHING
320 Broad Street
Red Bank, NJ 07701

First originally published by Newman Springs Publishing 2020

ISBN 978-1-63692-102-0 (Paperback)
ISBN 978-1-63692-103-7 (Digital)

Printed in the United States of America

To Cedric "Lil Ced, NIP" Pollard

ALL OR NOTHING

The ghetto is a low-income environment infested with drugs, gangs, corrupt police, poverty, and all the other circumstances conducive to hard living.

Roger "Mad Dog" Johnson is being raised in one such environment in Compton, California. In Compton, most youth find it almost impossible to avoid the seduction of gang life. Yet out of true determination some youngster defy the odds and persevere to live productive lives. However, most are born in the streets. Unless incarcerated, they will die in the same streets. Roger was raised in a single-parent home by a mother who worked hard to support three children. She also did her best to teach her children the values of education and productive living. However, Roger only saw life for what he saw in the neighborhood and chose street education over school education. Joining the local Crip gang was Roger's number one priority where he earned his stripes as Mad Dog.

(Can't Stop)

CHAPTER 1

On a hot Friday night in early July, Mad Dog was at home, preparing to go out and party with the homies at a spot in Watts. He returned home thirty minutes earlier to change clothes and give his mom part of the money he won in a dice game behind the central supermarket. Whenever possible, Mad Dog tried to help out the family financially. After Ms. Johnson had her youngest child, their father disappeared, leaving Mad Dog as the man of the house. Now dressed in freshly starched khakis and a crispy white tee, Mad Dog hopped in his gray-and-blue coup on hundred spokes deez headed for the Grandee where the Nutties hang. When he pulled up his comrade Ced, also dressed up for the function, greets, "What's up, my nigga?" In response, Mad Dog gave him the hood two-finger-and-a-thumb salute. After a brief thug hug, they stroll to the back carport where the rest of the locs were chilling and blowing trees before party time.

Hours later, riding up Wilmington listening to Scarface spit about made niggas. "Damn, cuz, I'm blowed," Mad Dog said, revealing he'd left his burner stashed in the gee'z.

"Don't trip, my nigga. I stay strapped," responded Ced. "Stop at the liquor store on Imperial so I can grab some blunts and OJ. My mouth dry as an old bitch pussy," he continued in a half-joking, half-serious way.

CHAPTER 2

Once in Watts, they pulled up in front of the Jordan Downs projects where tonight festivities are in full swing.

"It's a lot of mothafuckas cut here, cuz," Mad Dog said, "the rats look deeper than the niggas."

"Hell yea!" Ced excitedly replied. "But every time you put niggas and drinks together, some fool gone try to show out, especially on their turf," he continued. "So don't get to far away from a BG with those keys 'cause if I have to start dumpin'——ce lookin' to bounce quick. It's all G."

Mad Dog half laughed. "You always thinking the worst."

"Just stay focused," Ced shot back while exiting the car.

Inside, it was dark. After a brief pause by the door, the young men were able to see just how packed the little apartment was. There were people making out in the shadows while others were grinding on the dance floor to an oldie by Marvin Gaye.

"Oh yea, this is the business," said Mad Dog, ass overload. Look at how the honeys on us, bro. I'll be back."

Ced just shook his head and smiled as he watched his friend approach a group of ladies, thinking that fool's dick going to fall off as he continued to observe his surroundings. Finding a seat facing the front door to observe who came and left the party, Ced was about to fire up a blunt when he spotted a female resembling Mad Dog's little sister going in one of the rooms with an old head.

Sissy was thirteen but had the body of someone twice her age. With an ass to leaves little to the imagination, Mad Dog had to check plenty of niggas for trying to holla at his baby sister. However, she

8

never listened when he and Ms. Johnson tried to school her on the game men use to get the panties. Usually, she'd make fun of dog's protective ways. Now here, she is disappearing behind closed door with old cuz.

CHAPTER 3

On a mission to locate the homie and inform him of what I'd seen, I found cuz in the upstairs bathroom, receiving some head from some fat chick with pink hair. Even though Mad Dog gave me an evil stare once I got his attention, he excused himself from big moma's mouth, dried off with her shirt, and joined me in the hallway.

"Yea, cuz," Ced began, "I hate to fuck off your fun, but I thought you might be interested in knowing I just saw Sissy go in one of those downstairs rooms with some old head."

"Cuz, you trippin'!" Mad Dog hotly replied. "I just left Shawty at the pad with Mom and Lil Mark. Besides, what could she be doing way over here in the projects at night?"

"Hold up, my nigga," said Ced, holding up his hand and smiling. "Go see for yourself, cuz, on the set if—"

Ced never got to hear the rest 'cause Mad Dog was storming down the stairs in search of his little sister. There was only room on the lower level. Mad Dog rushed to the door, unprepared for what he saw. He entered and froze. All they could see was the back of a big black nigga with "Watts Life" tatted across it and equally huge arms wrapped around the waist of a female.

"Close that mothafuckin' door!" roared the big nigga, looking back to see who was hatin' on his fun.

Still frozen in place, Ced recognized the big dude as OG Vine from Grape Street Watts Crip gang. This recognition shocked the young loc at first. Ced apologized, "Sorry, big home. We were lookin' for someone I saw come through here."

"Well, as you can see," OG Vine roared, never missing a stroke, "it's only me and my bitch in here, so get out!"

With all the commotion in the room, the female turned to see what was going on. Sweaty, half naked, and obviously high, Sissy didn't recognize her brother at first glance. However, once she did, she tried to dislodge from OG Vine.

Not understanding what the deal was, Vine kept holding Sissy in a tight embrace and began to protest as one of the young dudes jumped on the bed. "What the fu—!" OG Vine began to say but was cut short by a vicious blow to the head.

Witnessing the drama unfold in her presence, Sissy scrambled to get dressed. Blind with rage, Mad Dog continued to rain blows to the face and head of Vine, all the time yelling, "I'mma kill you, fool!"

Being much bigger that the youth, Vine recovered fast and began returning blows and taking control of the situation. Upon seeing his home in trouble, Ced rushed to the assist him. Even two against one, they were no match for the OG. Remembering the strap on his hip, Ced backed up from the altercation, pulled his strap, and blasted Vine twice in his chest. The loud boom from the gun and Sissy's consistent screaming caused a crowd to gather at the door. Coming to his senses, Ced and Mad Dog grabbed sissy and ran from the apartment. As soon as they got outside, somebody started yelling behind them, "They shot Vine! They shot Vine!"

Just before they reached the parking lot, a man stepped in their path with intentions of stopping the three. Thinking quickly, Ced aimed midstride and shot the man down. Before anyone else can reach them, the teens got into the car and drove back to Compton, not understanding the effects their actions just created, actions that will change one of the strongest unions in gang history.

CHAPTER 4

Detective Swanson is a fifteen-year veteran of the Firestone Homicide Division. Having just closed the case of a domestic violence turned murder, he was dispatched to the scene of a double homicide on 101st Street in Watts. Detective Swanson and his partner is an odd team. Swanson, an average Caucasian man over fifty, was overweight, twice divorced, and counting the months till his retirement a year and a half away. His partner, on the other hand, grew up in the same projects he now patrolled. Detective Billy Joe Lockett joined the navy after high school and went on to become the first African American man to lead his naval tactical unit in a battle to reclaim Iraq's capital city. He later joined the Los Angeles police force with hopes of making the streets welcoming to all citizens, which is why when dispatched to a scene like that which he and his partner now faced was disappointing and personally sad. As they began investigating this present crime, Detective Lockett did most of the interviewing of anyone he could get to talk while Detective Swanson did his best to preserve any evidence of significance till the forensic team came.

"Man, I really dislike this shit," Lockett said, approaching his partner. "Will these children ever realize they are only hurting their own?"

Not an emotional man himself, Swanson simply shook his head. He and Lockett has been partners over ten years now so he was used to seeing Billy Joe's frustration over what he called black genocide. While first-response officers were updating the detectives on what they believed to have taken place at the party, Lockett excused himself to look at a group of bystanders. Before ever reaching the group, he spotted and smelled a neighborhood crackhead who goes by the moniker Mouse, probably because of his small beady eyes even when high on dope.

Knowing the detective was headed his way, Mouse put on a fake smile. "Boss man," Mouse greeted Lockett with even faker enthusiasm. "Long time no see."

"Yea," the detective countered, "I haven't saw you down in the bullpen lately." Although the cop knew it was a lie, he smiled when the drug addict said he was trying to clean up. Pulling Mouse to the side off to the left of the spectators. Reverting to the old street language, the detective asked Mouse, "What's the deal? What jumped off here tonight?"

"Shit, man! You know I don't fuck with others folks' business," Mouse said nervously.

The detective smirked, understanding the game the addict was playing. Often a dope fiend could be swayed to reveal information with small bribes or the threat of arrest when contraband is discovered on his or her person. Noticing the slight bulge in Mouse's pocket provoked the detective to grab him and put his hands on his head. In the pat down, the detective discovered a pipe used to smoke crack cocaine. Upon the discovery, Mouse began to speak fast and incomprehensively. Not willing to go back and forth with Mouse, the officer pulled out his cuffs and began to restrain the addict. By the time he was secured, Mouse was talking.

"Come on, brotha!" Mouse began. "I wasn't there. But from what I hear, some youngster shot big black over a girl!"

With a little more "encouragement," Detective Lockett also learned that the perpetrators drove off in a white Cadillac. Later, while sitting in their squad car, the two detectives were comparing notes. Along with the car the suspects fled in, they learned one of them wore a blue Compton ball cap, while the other had on a blue New York Yankees cap and jersey. The detectives, being knowledgeable of the Southern California gang culture, determined this case probably involved some form of gang activity.

CHAPTER 5

"Damb, cuz, you didn't have to blast the nigga!" Mad Dog said over emotional, as they drove in and out of traffic, still shaken up by what just took place.

Laughing and pulling on a freshly rolled blunt, Ced clowned. "Nigga, that old head was putting hands on our ass. I can't go out like that." He continued laughing. Cedric Smith was a tough little soldier from Nutty Blocc Compton Crip. Although he started bangin' later than Mad Dog, he already had a reputation for being quick on the trigger. As a matter of fact, rumors have it that he had multiple bodies under the belt. When his family moved from Texas to live in California, Cedric, a.k.a. Ced, was introduced to gangs, guns, and money. After his mother died of a stroke, he and his young brother Curtis was sent to live with his grandparent in Compton, California, one of the most violent cities in the country. Since their grandparents didn't have more than love to offer the boys, Ced took it upon himself to make sure he and Curtis had the things required to be comfortable.

Curtis, a.k.a. Lil Monsta, was also seduced by the lifestyle. Although he didn't sell drugs or carry a gun like his big brother, he was known throughout the neighborhood as a fuck up. On this night, tired after a day's mischief, Curtis was home sleep. On the other hand, Ced was headed back to the hood with a still hot 9mm Glock sitting on his lap. Mad Dog angrily eyed Sissy through the rearview mirror.

CHAPTER 6

The next morning, while Mad Dog was in his room, preparing the start of yet another day, Sissy came in.

"Roger," she began, "I'm sorry about yesterday."

Mad Dog, still angry and in shock from the discovery of his little sister's ways, continued about his business as if he didn't hear or see her.

"Come on, Rog," she continued in a whinny voice. "You know I wasn't trying to front you off, don't be mad.

Dog knew his sister was not a little bit sorry. She was only worried about their mother finding out. He finally spoke. "Sis, I'm not gone start preachin', we all get enough of that from Mom. But if you don't slow your roll, you gone end up like the rest of those ugly sluts you run with!"

"Boy, you crazy!" she replied with attitude as she stormed out the room.

In truth, Mad Dog probably should have paid more attention to his little sister 'cause no more than thirty minutes after leaving his room, Sissy and her hood rat friend Dallas were planning to catch a bus to Long Beach and meet up with some niggas they met at the mall last week.

On the other side of the hood on the six, Ced, as always in his yancee blue, was heading to the spot (drug house) in his '61 Chevy ragtop. He liked to serve early, believing the early-morning smokers trying to go up before work spend more.

The spot on Kemp Court was the plan, but as he pulled up, he saw the young loc Lil Crip Ced approached the car. He smiled, completely forgetting about crack and the crackheads. "West up?" he greeted the young soldier. "Ain't you supposed to be at school, nigga?"

Ced's brother was known around the hood as Lil Monsta. Ced and Mad Dog were best friends. Lil Crip Ced and Lil Monsta were also close.

As a reply to his older homie's question, Lil Crip Ced said, "I'm not going today. Pop's acting like a bitch, and I need some doe (money). Can I hang with you today?"

"That's cool," Ced said. "Hop in."

The two drove off with Tupac's "Hail Mary" bumpin' from the expensive sound system.

CHAPTER 7

In the projects, word spread about OG Vine getting shot last night. People gathered together at a spot in the new homes. A group of influential Watts soldiers was trying to put down a plan for retaliation for the death of their comrade. Amongst these individuals are Big Ryda from Santa Ana Watergate and Young Bo from the Imperial Courts projects.

"Cuz, fuck that!" Ryda was saying. "I got supa love one's from the hub, and I can't believe they would have shit to do with this."

"Nigga," Bo countered, "you ain't even from Watts, so why you got anything to say about it?"

Ryda supplied the guns to most of the Crip gangs in Southern California under the impression that his supplies are not used in Crip-on-Crip violence. "Fool you from the PJs," Ryda countered.

"So why are you here?"

"Y'all niggas need to chill the fucc out!" Someone else in the room interrupted the two arguing. We're here to get to the bottom of this shit, not create more drama amongst ourselves. Real talk," Ray dog said, "I got much love for the hub. I'm going to cut there today and holla at some people about a white lac and the NY hat. I know the nutty's bang the NY in Compton."

Ryda spoke up. "If we can find out who the bitch was, we would probably find out who the fools were she left with."

After discussing a few more details, the small group began to disperse, destined for a couple different destinations yet searching for one answer. Who shot Vine. A few young soldiers in the room, like their older homies, had plans of their own.

Infant Bay Nutt, in his own right, was known as a shooter. While sitting amongst the OGs, practically unnoticed, he saw this situation as an opportunity to build on his growing reputation. The way he rationalized his plan was, if the Nutty Blocc was responsible for capping the big homie, he intended to cap on some nutties.

CHAPTER 8

While Ced and Mad Dog were in the spot, counting the profit from the morning drug traffic, Lil Monsta, Lil Crip Ced, and the third piece to their cicle of TG's yung criccet were out front, clownin' around while keeping their eyes open for the narcs. The young homies regularly earned some dollas by being the watch out boys when the spot was in business. However, on this day, unaware of any danger, the three TGs laughed and joked with each other as an unknown assassin made ready to change their young lives forever.

CHAPTER 9

Infant Nutt sat low in the G-ride (stolen car), watching three young niggas and waiting to see the white Cadillac with an AK-47 laid across his lap. He already concluded that if push came to shove, he would air out the little dudes before leaving. Though not fully remembering all the details he heard earlier in the meeting, he did recognize one of the niggas down the street was wearing a blue Yankees ball cap. So he sat watching and waiting, noting the flow of traffic until the sky began darkening.

CHAPTER 10

After getting shit in order inside the spot, Ced was preparing to leave. He's been trappin' since before noon. Now out of product, he was thinking of only one thing, Kim's pussy. Kim was a redbone tender he met one day at Roscoe's. She had a freaky side that never failed to bring a loc back for more. He was anticipating a long night of uncut fuckin'.

"Damb, cuz," Mad Dog said, interrupting his thoughts. "I see Kim got yo ass whipped," he joked laughing.

"Fool, be real," Ced shot back, realizing he was caught daydreaming. "Unlike you, nigga, I can't put my dick in no smoker pussy." He went on, "Hell yea! The pussy's good, but the mouth's six times better."

They both fell out laughing to that, slappin' hands, and enjoying the statement.

"Well, you know how the OBG get it, Crip," Mad Dog said, not willing to let his comrade get the last word, stick and move.

With that statement, they began a whole new round of laughter.

After a minute more of clownin' around, Ced said, "Well, let me bounce 'cause G mom will kick an OBG's ass if I keep lil bro out past cuz streetlights curfew."

Outside, Ced stood on the porch, observing the three young homies for a minute before calling out to his brother. "Monsta!" he yelled. "Let go my nigga!"

Before his brother or his friends could respond, a car came creeping down the block without lights. Not recognizing the car, Ced started running to the yard and pulled his strap. Before he could make his move, however, gunfire erupted from the old Regal aimed toward the young ones.

CHAPTER 11

Infant Nutt finally decided to make his move. Tired of waiting, he checked the weapon before pulling away from the curb, remembering to leave off the car lights so he would not to be noticed before he could carry out his intent. Slowly creepin', he noticed an older teen come out a house, speaking to the boys. He was running in their direction and looking his way. Believing he was spotted, he sped up, pulling parallel to the boys. As one of the youngsters looked up, Infant Nutt stepped out of the car and fired.

Two of the boys dove to the ground. A split-second hesitation put the third one directly in the line of fire. He was hit multiple times from the automatic weapon's bullet's, Infant Nutt's instinct was to back to the car and go after the other two, but the guy from the house was running in his direction, armed with his own weapon. Thinking one is better than none, he jumped back in his ride, speeding toward Ced who was getting closer by the second. Trying to run down Ced instead of just leaving was a mistake. Not only did he miss, but in the few seconds he wasted, he realized too late that it would cost him his own young life.

From the moment Ced saw the strange car stop and a nigga jumping out to blast his homies, he was determined to get the perpetrator, running at full speed and preparing to blast caps of his own. He saw the car speeding directly toward him and had to dive out of the way before getting off a shot. However, growing up in the hood, Ced knew that the two blocks were connected so the car had to exit from only one end. Ignoring the need to check on his brother and friends, Ced was looking to meet the assassin who was trying to exit to the next street. Running all out, he reached his destination, readying his 9mm Glock to do the rest.

CHAPTER 12

O nce rounding the bend, Infant Nutt realized he'd be exiting from only one street over from the shooting. Nevertheless, he saw no one pursuing him so he proceeded to the end of the street, believing he was getting away. Then he looked back one time before Ced unleashed a full clip of .45-caliber hollow-point bullets at his car.

Before he fully understood that the end was near, he felt the first of many slugs tearing through his body. As a matter of fact, long before the clip was empty, the car was slowly rolling forward with Infant Nutt's dead body slumped across the front seat.

CHAPTER 13

Running up on the car, Ced knew that after seeing the body, there was nothing more he could do there. His thoughts turned toward the welfare of his little brother and young homies. By the time he got back to the scene, the first thing he noticed was the shocked look on his brother and Lil Crip Ced's face as they stood amongst the crowd standing around the body of cricket.

Walking up, Ced pulled the two youngsters back to the spot to where Mad Dog was. He was standing in the yard, discretely holding a large gun of his own, prepared for anything else that might come.

Back inside the spot, the two TGs started talking. Death was normal in the ghetto. This was evident as the youngsters replayed the activities to their OBGs in a calm, almost detached way.

CHAPTER 14

Hearing about the murder in Compton a couple of days later, Detectives Swanson and Lockett of the LAPD believed this could possibly be in some way connected with the project homicides on a hunch. When the information gathered in their own investigation revealed nothing, Detective Lockett was concerned. After the regular morning briefing in the conference room, Lockett expressed to his partner his thoughts and suggested they visit Compton Police Department to see if they could get some guidance from its own string of recent homicides.

"Do you think there's a connection there?" Detective Swanson asked his partner.

"Can't hurt to compare notes," Lockett responded. "Besides, if I sit behind this desk another day without some action, my ass will grow warts."

Laughing at his partner's choice of reasoning, Swanson grabbed his coat as a signal to Lockett's hunch. "Let's do this."

Later at the CPD, the two detectives met up with Sergeant Booker and were escorted upstairs to the Homicide Division. Sergeant Booker had also been concerned with the two murders recently committed. Last year, Compton had one of the highest murder rates in the United States. Already only three months into the year, they had fifty-one unsolved homicides. After proper introductions, the men sit and converse about the issue, learning that one of the bodies was traced through prints to an address in Watts, which made this encounter even more interesting. Detective Lockett revealed his suspicious that brought them to Compton. "Yes, we had a double homicide last week." Through an informant, they learned that one of the suspects wore a ball cap with "Compton" stitched across the front.

"Shit!" said Sergeant Booker. "That could be any number of knuckleheads running around the city."

"Yes, sir, I considered that too. However, the second suspect was also wearing a ball cap, except it was of the New York Yankees," offered Swanson.

Pausing to contemplate momentarily, Booker thought out loud, "That rings familiar. Excuse me, gentlemen. Let me run this by one of my guys in gang prevention."

Almost as fast as he left, Sergeant Booker returned with another officer named Smults. Smults was a part of a task unit in Compton similar to the LAPD's crash unit. Gang prevention task (GPT) force's main objective was to slow down the gang activity in the city.

After exchanging greetings, Officer Smults said, "Oh yea, we have some fellas out here that favor those particular caps, and they're a real thorn in our ass." He continued looking through his files. "Okay, here we go. Nutty Blocc Crips! Unusual name, but I've had the pleasure—or should I say, unpleasure—of crossing paths with these boys. And let me tell you, hey a bunch of assholes. Had a case last year where a group of them beat up and raped a young lady for simply wearing red to school in their neighborhood."

As the officer talked, Swanson took noted, and his partner sat a little shocked as he tried to visualize such characters. After discussing a few more details regarding the gang, the LAPD detectives thanked Booker and Smults, leaving with a new hope on their case.

CHAPTER 15

For weeks, Mad Dog couldn't stop thinking about the drama that has recently engulfed his peace. It really worried him most after criccet was killed 'cause his gut told him it was a result of what happened at the Watts party. He began looking over his shoulder.

"Damn!" he said to himself. "This shit got me trippin'."

All over Sissy ass and she's still running wild. But even now he had no idea just how wild or he'd probably have not been so shocked of her actions the night of the party.

At that very moment, Mad Dog was lost in his thoughts, Sissy and her best friend Dallas were back in Watts, unaware of the danger that would soon invade their lives.

CHAPTER 16

"Girl, you sure those niggas is paid?" asked Dallas as they walked down Imperial Bird.

"I already told you," Sissy said, answering back with attitude, "I've been here before. Bitch, you worry too much. You'll see. These old niggas got money, and they're dumb enough for us to get it." She smiled.

"I just wish we would have called first," Dallas mumbled.

Turning into a driveway of their destination, both girls were relieved. Before they could reach the front door, it came open and a rough-looking brotha came out, smiling. "Look here, look here," he said, rubbing his hands together, "young pussy!"

As Sissy smiled, Dallas was beginning to second-guess her decision to come along with her friend. Once inside, the rough-looking brotha name Spook, a moniker from his dark complexion, made drinks before rollin' some blunts.

"Shit, boo!" Spook said, sipping his gin and coke. "If I knew you were coming, I'd have picked you up somewhere." Turning toward Dallas with lust in his eyes, he continued, "And some Viagra." He laughed at his own words.

Again, Dallas was regretting coming. Sissy, on the other hand, was a greedy slut. All she could see was dollars as she sat on the man's lap, who was three times her age. She purred, grinding her shapely ass on his already hardening dick.

"Go and fire up the weed, daddy, so we can get this party started."

CHAPTER 17

M ad Dog noticed the unmarked police car a couple of days ago and told Ced he thought the spot was being watched. Long forgotten about the situation in Watts since death was a normal activity in the ghetto, Ced and Mad Dog shut down operations at the spot, believing drugs was the reason for the police interest. However, now aware as they began seeing the cop car throughout the hood, Ced expressed one day, "Cuz, the hood is hot. I think we should lay low."

So, they found an apartment in Long Beach and avoided the streets as much as possible.

CHAPTER 18

The information Detectives Lockett and Swanson received from the CPD was slowly paying off. A week or so ago, they decided to use some of their downtime to drive out to the neighborhood occupied by the Nutty Blocc gang. They were not expecting much, just observing. They made the drive a few time, even venturing over in the evening after regular work hours.

Then one afternoon, while waiting in their car on Central Avenue and Alondra Boulevard for the red light, they spotted a white Cadillac that fit the description given by a witness the day of the shooting in Watts.

"Well, look at that!" Swanson pointed out to his partner.

Following his partner's gaze, Lockett saw what caught his attention. "Could be," he said. "Let's follow him."

Making a quick U-turn, the detectives proceeded to trail the white car that just left the parking lot of Walters market. They followed it to a rundown house on 166th Street then to another one in the same neighborhood on Kemp Court. Seeing a young black teenager enter the house, they parked down the block where they could observe from a distance. However, when the teenager failed to exit after some time, Swanson logged the address and left, deciding to follow up on their hunch the next day. Swanson also noticed the foot traffic coming and going from the residence.

The next day, the detectives were back. Parked at the far end of Kemp Court, watching the white Cadillac return.

"There's our friend," said Lockett with a bit of excitement in his voice after a couple of hours of boredom.

Although they saw the car make brief stops, the young man in the white Cadillac appeared to have the air of authority at the house, even the crackheads became more animated seeing the teen. Then all of a sudden, the atmosphere changed after a couple days when things slowed down drastically. By the end of the week, the only people coming or going from the house was the two young men in the Cadillac. The two detectives still didn't have anything solid, except the alleged getaway car, so Swanson made the suggestion of bring a witness to see if they could get a positive identification at least on the car. However, by Monday, the street had suddenly gone quiet. Not only did the car with the two young men stop coming around, but the house looked abandoned.

Could the detectives have been seen, wondered Lockett. "Damn!" he mumbled under his breath as he drove slowly past the house.

Loss in thought, both men were silent on the ride back to their police station, not understanding and perhaps a little angry. Detectives Swanson and Lockett wondered how they could have let an easy lead slip away. Their captain had already been on their ass about neglecting the other cases on their desk. Time was running short.

CHAPTER 19

The same day, Sissy and her friend Dallas spent entertaining Spook was the same day she was recognized by a guy who remembered seeing her with OG Vine the day he was killed. He also remembered the talk in the streets about two niggas who fled with a female after the shooting and could only assume she was the one. He spoke to his homie. "Peep cuz, that's the bitch I saw with Vine."

Looking at what caught his rade's attention, Sweet Pea instructed Lil Cee, the driver, and his day one loc, to follow the girls. They trailed them to a bus stop and decided to see just where the girls get off. Upon entering the city of Compton, the girls got off in a residential area, unaware that they were being stalked.

Heading in separate directions, Lil Cee and Sweet Pea paid little attention to the unknown female except to admire her ass as she walked away. Their focus was on Sissy. As the young men crept along, observing their surroundings, they saw how busy the area was. Trying to look as if they belong, they avoided eye contact with any of the people and focused on not losing Sissy. The plan in Lil Cee's mind was to grab the girl, but before a promising opportunity came, she turned into the yard of a rundown house. Once she went in, she didn't emerge. The two youths left and vowed to return to finish what they started, not even realizing just how simple the task would be.

CHAPTER 20

Mad Dog and Ced had been laying low for a couple of weeks and was becoming bored and restless. Although neither one had the desire to return to the spot on Kemp Court, they felt the need to get out and check on some things. Except by phone calls, neither one had been home or even to the hood since temporarily shutting down the spot. Without the cash flow, shit was getting tight. So on Wednesday, with the weather hot as hell, they decided to go handle some business and meet up later.

While preparing to leave, Mad Dog was saying to his homie, "Yea cuz, I'm gone slide by Mom's and check in."

"I feel you, my nigga," Ced responded. "I'll be through the hood later after I holla at my girl."

With that, he left, leaving Mad Dog.

CHAPTER 21

Once the LAPD detectives realized the house on Kemp was no longer occupied, they began to focus on the other homes the white car visited. After watching this one specific home for a couple of days without any sign of their suspects, the two maintained hope. Unlike the other home believed to be a drug den, this home was occupied by a family of three: an older lady, a teenage girl, and a young boy.

Today they decided to inquire about the individual who drove the Cadillac. The young boy answered the door after a couple of knocks. "What's up?" he asked, looking the men up and down.

"Hi!" Detective Lockett greeted the young man with a smile. Is your mother or father home?"

"Hold up," Lil Crip Ced said, slamming the door in their faces.

"Friendly," Swanson said under his breath.

A short time later, the elderly lady opened the door. "Yes, may I help you?"

"Hello, ma'am," Lockett began. "Actually, we're not sure if you can assist us or not, but we're LAPD detectives, following up on information regarding a vehicle seen here a couple weeks ago."

"Go on," she said, not bothering to hide the contempt in her voice or extending the curtesy of coming into the house, out the heat.

"Well," Lockett continued, "we followed a white Cadillac to your residence and was hoping to ask the driver some questions, if that's possible."

This got her attention 'cause she finally opened the door wider and asked the detectives to come in. Once inside, Ms. Johnson explained that her oldest son drove the white car. "Is he in some kind of trouble, officer?" she asked, concern in her voice.

Not wanting to reveal more than necessary, Detective Lockett replied, "No, ma'am! We're just looking to ask him a couple of questions."

Clutching the cross attached to a chain around her neck, Ms. Johnson informed them that her son hadn't been over in a few weeks. "You still ain't telling me what this is all about."

"Mrs. Johns—"

"That's Miss," she corrected him.

"Sorry, Ms. Johnson. As I said before, our intention is only to question your son about an incident that took place a few weeks ago."

Tired of the word play, Ms. Johnson escorted the detectives to the door. "Well, gentlemen, as I told you, Rodger has not been by."

Realizing this was a signal to leave, the detective extended a card to the mother, asking that if she saw her son, give him a call.

"I'll do that," she said, closing the door almost on their heels.

"Damn!" Detective Swanson began once back in their car. "That was one tough lady."

Those were the first words he spoke during the entire visit.

CHAPTER 22

Yesterday, Sissy acted as though she didn't notice the car following her home from school. However, she made sure she added a little extra swing in her hips. Today, as she stood at the checkout counter of the neighborhood store, she saw the same car. Again, they were checking her out. Not being unusual for both boys and men to pay her attention, she decided to see if she could have some fun and even a few dollars from their interest.

Upon leaving the store, she walked right up to the driver side window and leaned in, making sure she revealed a promising view of her cleavage. "Hi!" she said with enthusiasm. "You staring like you see something tasty," she flirted.

Caught by surprise, it took Lil Cee a couple seconds to retort. "Yea, boo. We saw all that ass and couldn't look away."

"Like that?" She smiled.

With only a few more exchange of words, Sissy was sitting in the front seat between Lil Cee and Sweet Pea. Sissy was the type of young girl who liked to party. She didn't care where she went or with whom. She was down for whatever. He motto was "Have fun while you're young."

CHAPTER 23

Mad Dog stopped by his mother's house Friday night to check on the family. Before he could make it to the door though, his little brother cut him short and told him about the police coming by, looking for him. "What they say?" he inquired.

However, unable to gain much insight from the conversation, Mad Dog went inside to speak about it with his mom to figure out what's up. Finding his mother in the kitchen, preparing dinner as usual at his hour of day, he snuck up on her with a big playful kiss on her cheek.

Giggling like a schoolgirl, Ms. Johnson turned to her oldest child, smiling while shooing him away with her cooking towel. "Boy, you better get away from me!" She continued giggling. Looking every bit of his teenage years, Ms. Johnson loved the close relationship she shared with her firstborn.

"What's up, sexy?" he teased.

She said, still smiling, "Boy, between you and your sister, y'all gone drive me crazy."

Even with the smile, Roger could hear the stress in his mom's voice. Frowning, he asked, "What's up, Momma? Talk to me."

Sitting down with a sigh and welcoming the opportunity to reveal her concerns, Ms. Johnson began to express her concerns regarding her children. "Well," she began, "I don't know what to do with your sister. The school has been calling about her missing school." Her smile was replaced with sadness.

"Where she at?" Mad Dog asked angrily.

"Boy, I don't know! But I'm the parent here, and I'll deal with her. What's this mess with you and the police?" Her attention was firmly directed toward him. "They come here asking about your car. You in some trouble?"

"No, ma'am," he answered.

"Don't you lie to me, Roger!"

"No, for real, Mom! I don't know what that's about."

She gave him the card she got from them. Trying hard to hide his worry, Mad Dog took the card, cutting his visit shorter than intended. Before making it out the door though, he heard his mom say, "If you see your fast-tailed sister, send her ass home."

Although concerned about the reason for the police visit, Roger was upset with the news of his sister. He was on his way to find her and kick her ass. After driving around for more than a couple of hours, he couldn't find Sissy anywhere, which only heightened his anger. Around ten o'clock, he called his mom's house and learned from his brother that she had shown up yet. Continuing to check out all the hangouts frequently visited by both teens and adults in the city, Mad Dog still hadn't found his little sister. Knowing what he did about her reputation, he decided she was somewhere slutting around and went on to take care of his own business before meeting back up with his homie Ced.

CHAPTER 24

Ced, on the other hand, was spending some well needed time with his girl, Kim. Before taking the time off from the spot, Ced left some product (crack) with his brother, Lil Monsta. So after going to get his money, his next stop was her apartment. Now some four or five hours after arriving, he was feeling refreshed and ready to see what Mad Dog had on the agenda for the night.

Kim, not having seen Ced in weeks, also loved the quality time with her man. Therefore, when he started preparing to leave, she began to protest, but Ced promised they would be together all weekend. This did please and sound promising to Kim.

As Ced drove back to Compton, he was still smiling from his time with his boo and the thought of a whole weekend together.

CHAPTER 25

S issy realized she was in over her head when she mentioned to Lil Cee that she had to get home. She'd been with him and Sweet Pea for several hours now. As the time got later, she knew her mother would be really upset when she got home. True, she did enjoy kicking it with the two young men and even assured them they could continue another day. She also began getting a strange vibe now that the fun was over. Their moods went from lust to what seemed like distaste now, even hate. The look in their eyes seemed evil, and she couldn't understand why. She'd done everything they asked of her without hesitation. She paid little attention on the way over here and did not know where she was. Add to that the hour and change in attitude of the boys, she was getting scared. She went to Cee again, trying to plead her case.

"Look, Cee, baby," she began, "if I don't show up soon, my mother will be trippin' and calling all my friends. Trying to follow me to school and shit." She laughed, hoping to change the mood in the room.

Sweet Pea only stared at her for a minute. "Look, bitch! Sit yo ass down! We'll drop you off when we're ready." Sissy was about to respond but was cut short by a vicious slap. "Bitch, I said kick back before you get hurt!"

Holding her face and putting some distance between her and him, she was still confused about the sudden aggression. Not wanting to be hit again, she followed orders. It was not until around four o'clock that the young men were ready to go. Sissy had fallen asleep and was woken up by a blow to the side of her head. "Let's roll!" was all she heard as the men led the way out to the car.

Once inside, the only thing to remedy the silence was the rap music coming from the speakers. On the highway, she noticed they were going in the wrong direction. With every passing second, Sissy was regretting ever meeting Lil Cee and Sweet Pea. She'd been used and abused. She just wanted to get home. All the nagging she received from her mother over the years now replayed in her mind, and she regret not listening. As they drove in to a secluded area of downtown that was full of abandoned warehouses, she began looking for the opportunity to escape. The bad vibes continued, and the fear increased tenfold.

When they stopped, she jumped out all of a sudden. She started running and yelling desperately for help! However, before she could get a good ten yards, Sweet Pea stepped out from the passenger side of the vehicle and shot her in the back without hesitation. Sissy went down hard, but the adrenaline and fear had her crawling foolishly. In reality, she knew the effort was useless, but the sound of the young men laughing behind her wouldn't let her just give up. Finally, with nowhere to go, she was forced to stop.

While Lil Cee went to the trunk of the car, his partner walked over her, still smiling. With eyes blurry from her tears, all the girl could do was cry harder as Lil Cee joined Sweet Pea, holding a gas can. "Well, well, well," Cee said. If it ain't the little slut from the party with Vine. Remember that, bitch!" he yelled, kicking her in the ass. "Now I need to know who the nigga is that killed the homie?"

Already accepting her fate, and with the mention of that terrible day, Sissy knew she'd never leave there alive. She'd never see her family again, and the fun times of her youth was over. In her only selfless act in life, she refused to betray her brother. He was always trying to help her. She couldn't bring any more pain to the ones she loved.

"Bitch, you hear me talking?" Cee continued as he kicked her again. She just laid there in pain, crying.

Seeing she was not going to cooperate and not wanting to get caught if the cop's rolled through, Lil Cee poured the gas on the girl, completely soaking her. As he went in his pocket for a match, Sweet

Pea spat in her face and shot her twice in the head at close range. Before returning to his vehicle, Lil Cee tossed a lit match on the body.

By dawn, the factory workers discovered what looked like the charcoaled remains of a body.

CHAPTER 26

C ed and Mad Dog was hungover and tired from clubbing late. When the phone started ringing around nine o'clock, both boys tried to ignore it. However, the ringing was consistent. Unable to go back to sleep, Ced finally went to answer the phone on the living room couch. When he picked it up, he recognized his young homie and Mad Dog's brother. Lil Crip Ced sounded as if he was crying, which made it almost impossible to understand what he was saying.

Fully awake now, Ced tried to calm the youngster down so he could make some sense of what he was being saying, "Cuz! Cuz!" It was a while before Lil Crip Ced was able to speak with some clarity. Afterward, Ced could only stand shocked before going to get Mad Dog.

Hearing all the loud talk though, Mad Dog already pulled himself out his bed. They met in the hall where all Ced could do was hand him the cell and rush to get dressed. "What's up?" he spoke into the phone. He just listened as his brother managed to get out his message. "I'm on my way!" was all Mad Dog could say as he hung up. With legs too weak to stand, he sat down and cried.

"Ain't no time for that, loc," Ced said as he returned to the living room, smoking on a blunt. "Let's bounce."

That pulled Mad Dog back to the present. When he finally joined Ced in the car, he had an AK-47 in one hand and an AR-15 semiautomatic rifle in the other.

Ced drove off, lost in his own thoughts.

CHAPTER 27

The burned-up body of a young female was all over the news. Because of the condition of the body, it was impossible to identify. It was now sitting at the coroner's office where they intended to see if there was enough of the teeth to possibly identify the Jane Doe. The crime itself sparked outrage among the media and community. The amber alert was asking if anyone could provide any information regarding the crime or missing reports filed to please contact (1-800-WeTip). Homicide and arson detectives had been searching the area for hours, even knocking on doors of the few residence in the vicinity.

KCAP anchorwoman Debra Jacobs was live. "We're here at the clown toy factory in Downtown Los Angeles," she was saying, "where a horrific crime has happened in the early hours of the morning. What appeared to be the burned remains of a female body was discovered by the manager of the business. Already you can see a few flowers has been laid at the scene where the Jane Doe was found. Anyone with information can contact us here at KCAP. All calls are confidential so please call 1-976-KCAPNews or 1-800-WeTip. Once again, we're live at the scene of a sad crime, I'm Debra Jacobs, live."

Across the city, Mad Dog turned off the TV and just sat with his head down. He and Ced had been at his mother's house after receiving the call from his brother. Since their sister never came home, they could only assume, although they hope not, that the person in the news was Sissy.

Although concerned about her daughter not coming home last night, Ms. Johnson knew the truth that her daughter was loose. She did try to keep her in line, but working two jobs and with a young son to worry about, she did all she could. Leaving before the breaking news broadcast, she was unaware of the events unfolding, and her son's didn't want to stress her before knowing for a fact that their suspicion was true.

"Damn, cuz! I have a fucked-up feeling about this," Mad Dog spoke out loud to no one in particular. Being the oldest sibling, he knew he had to be the one to reveal his thoughts to his mother first with the help of his best friend. He spent close to an hour calling around, trying to see if, by some miracle, she was with a friend. Yet by midday, he was forced to interrupt his mother's work.

With tears and a heavy heart, she called the Compton Sheriff Department and reported her daughter missing. After explaining her concerns, they promised to ignore the normal twenty-four-hour protocol to file the report. When Ms. Johnson got home, she was both emotionally and physically drained. Her sons were hanging out, and the atmosphere was gloomy, which only added to her sadness. However, no one was willing to speak about their situation.

After about an hour without any news, Mad Dog gave his mother a long hug. "Mom, if anything comes up, have bro call me. I'm gone ride around some."

She just hugged him harder and said, "Be careful."

As they drove through the city, Mad Dog told Ced, "Cuz, ever since Lil Cricket was gunned down, now this shit with Sis, I think it's got something to do with the drama at the party. My gut tells me they behind this. Yea, I know those the homies, but this got personal."

"Say no more, my nigga," Ced responded. "Let's go do a nutty on those clowns."

CHAPTER 28

The two LA homicide detectives had begun to believe they would never catch a good enough lead to close the double homicide a couple of weeks back. As a last-ditch effort, they decided to visit the residence in Compton and follow up on the white Cadillac. They arrived around dinner and had an interesting conversation with a tearful Ms. Johnson who explained the disappearance of her daughter.

"My baby's missing!" she managed to say. "She never came home last night, and the possibility of her being the person mentioned on the news got my nerves." Unable to speak further, she fell into another fit of crying.

Detectives Lockett and Swanson was also able to learn how upset her oldest son had been when he left. On the drive back to their department, the two detectives, each in his own head, was wondering if this latest incident could somehow be connected to their case.

CHAPTER 29

M ad Dog and Ced rolled around the city, hoping to find out one last time if any of Sissy friends heard from her. Without any positive results, anger was taking over, and the young men decided to go to the projects. As they drove down Compton Avenue, they noticed various activities around the rival gang neighborhood. Seeing this as an opportunity, they were immediately distracted from their original destination.

"Cuz, look at all these slobs!" Ced stated excitedly.

Lost in his own thoughts, Mad Dog had not even been aware of his surroundings. Ced's voice snapped him back to reality. He too noticed all the people. "Damn, cuz, look at all these slobs!"

"Nigga, I just said that."

Circling the block, the young men parked down the block to further observe. Having been friends since preteen, both young men usually shared similar thoughts about the gang lifestyle. Now was no different. With all the other drama in his life, Mad Dog saw this as an opportunity to vent.

"What you wona do, my nigga?" Ced asked, reading Mad Dog's mind. Even as he was asking, he reached over the back seat to retrieve the weapon he kept stashed under the cushion.

Mad Dog also removed his gun from his waist and was checking to make sure it was functional. Satisfied, he looked over to his partner and comrade. "Let's do this!"

Ced's only reply was a brief smirk as he eyed a group of men on the corner of 113th Street. Now cruising in that direction, Ced rolled down his window as Mad Dog sat low in his seat, waiting for them to pull over. The group on the corner, comfortable in their hood, didn't pay any attention to the white Cadillac that stopped a couple of houses down from where they were hangin' out, passing a bottle of liquor around and clownin'. They never gave a first or second glance in that direction when the two figures left the car and began walking toward them.

CHAPTER 30

Mad Dog and Ced left their car and began to approach the guys on the corner. The guys, lost in their fun times and intoxication, failed to notice when Ced reached under his jacket and produced his weapon. Mad Dog left the car with his gun already in hand, walking faster.

As one of the young men finally glanced over, it was already too late. Gunshots rang out! Even as the sound of bullets sobered up the young blood gang members, fear left them frozen in place, and the automatic weapon did the rest. Almost as soon as the shooting began, it stopped. The bodies of the men who, only seconds ago, were enjoying their day, were laid out, dead.

Dog and Ced, having relieved some stress, calmly walked back to their car and drove away.

CHAPTER 31

The local news began the morning with a number of hot topics. The vicious slaying in Watts had the gang unit crash up all night, pulling over cars and snatching every suspected gang member off the streets foolish enough to be out after the shooting. Through dental records, the unidentified Jane Doe found burned to death in an industrial area of Los Angeles was identified. No names were released because all victims from both incidents were juvenile at their morning briefing. Detectives Lockett and Swanson received this same information at their desk. The two were debating the possibility of the recent string of violence being connected. They made calls to other precincts, trading and comparing notes of recent violent crimes. The results all came back to the same thing, the white Cadillac. Deciding they had enough of a hunch to share their suspicion with the captain, the detectives gathered their file and set out for his office.

Captain Smith was a cranky fat man, disgruntled and hardened from his thirty-plus years as an LAPD street cop. The majority of his coworkers considered him an asshole because of his attitude. The detectives knew they had to be right.

"Good morning, Windy," Detective Lockett greeted the secretary. "The boss man in?"

Smiling at the handsome black detective, Windy replied, as she left her desk, making sure to add some extra swings to her hips. All Lockett could do was lick his lips. "Go right in," Windy said upon returning.

Entering Captain Smith's office, the detectives took the chairs in front of his desk.

"What can I do for you, gentlemen? Need more work?" he questioned in his dry humor.

The detectives shared a quick glimpse to each other before they began telling their theory regarding the case of the party in Watts. They didn't want to overstep their jurisdiction and was seeking advice on how to pursue. Considering the murder of the teenage female was radiating some real heat from the government, the captain made a few calls and promised the detectives, he'd get back a little of both disappointment and hope. The detective left Captain Smith's office.

CHAPTER 32

While Ced was laying low at the Long Beach spot, Mad Dog was at his mother's house, trying to comfort her in her grief. Although he felt good about the work he put in the previous night, the pain he saw in his mother's eyes was an indication that he was not done. His little brother was also beginning to act out, which was a major concern for Roger, considering the condition of Sissy's remains. Rodger (Mad Dog) and Ms. Johnson decided to cremate the body and hold a celebratory wake to honor her life with family and friends. As the day grew late, Mad Dog's mind was occupied with the coming activities scheduled for the weekend.

CHAPTER 33

Captain Smith succeeded in obtaining an arrest warrant for Roger Johnson. Detectives Swanson and Lockett made plans to make yet another trip to Compton. It was a fairly nice day as the surveillance van parked down the block from 1703 West 166th Street. Aware that Roger did not live with his mother, the detectives believed that because of the wake, this could be their chance to run into the suspect. There was already quite a bit of activity at the residence. They stayed alert and hoped to spot the white Cadillac.

Mad dog and Ced was also up early, preparing for the day's activities.

"Cuz, I don't like this shit," Mad Dog said from the kitchen. "I barely slept, seeing Mom's grief."

"Shit, I can't fully understand your pain, loc, but you're my nigga, and I'll be here for you through this," Ced responded. Trying to lighten the mood, Ced gave a little laugh and continued. "It's a blunt you can fire up on top of the microwave. That white willow will also help."

"Whatever, nigga," Mad Dog shot back as he lit the blunt and took a deep pull. Blowing out a huge smoke cloud, he continued. "Crip, don't you think it's strange how quiet it's been after we laid those slobs?"

"What you expect to be happening, my nigga? They don't know we did that," Ced said.

"I'm just saying I got a funny feeling," Mad Dog replied, taking another deep pull of the potent weed. He couldn't put a finger on it, but he had a feeling.

CHAPTER 34

Hours into the surveillance, the two detectives from LA was joined by two Compton detectives for jurisdictional purposes, also with unsolved homicides of their own. This could bring a resolution to this issue.

As it got closer to the scheduled time for the wake, activity at the Johnson home increased. People and cars came and left, except for the intended target. Then out of nowhere, the white Cadillac came cruising down 166th Street. When the officers recognize the vehicle, excited energy could be felt amongst them.

"There goes our perp," Detective Swanson stated as a fact but to no one directly.

"He's not alone," one of the other detectives noticed.

"Damn," Swanson continued, "this could be a problem."

"Man, they don't know we're here. We have the element of surprise on our side," his partner interjected. "Let's just move in fast."

"Sound's good to me."

"Me too," the Compton detectives agreed.

As the Cadillac pulled into the yard of the home, the squad car sped toward its target. Then all hell broke loose.

CHAPTER 35

As Mad Dog drove down the block, he noticed how calm it was. "Cuz," he said to his comrade, "I thought it would be hella cars at the house." Glancing down at his watch, he realized it was the time. "It's almost one," he informed Ced. "Most of the fam must be at the church."

As he pulled up in his mom's yard, his little brother ran from the house with Ms. Johnson also coming out to greet her son. Like a scene from a movie, as the two young men exited, the car police seem to have come from the sky.

"Get down! Get down!" the officers yelled, running up with guns drawn.

"Freeze!" the officer closest to one to the boys ordered.

Though caught off guard, it only took a second for Mad Dog and Ced to react. With Ms. Johnson screaming from the porch and her youngest son caught in the middle of the drama, the distraction gave Ced an opportunity to run toward the front door. Ms. Johnson was still screaming hysterically on the porch when Ced reached to retrieve the weapon concealed in his waist and fired multiple shots at the officers. It hit one detective in the face who went down hard.

Entering the house, Ced never slowed as he ran through the living room and out the back door by the kitchen. At the same time, Mad Dog was still out front. Caught on the opposite side of the car, he found himself out in the open, directly in the line of fire. However, with the excitement caused by Ced, Mad Dog reached back for his own gun in the driver's seat and came out blasting off a few slugs of his own.

"Die, pig!" he yelled as one of the slugs hit Detective Swanson in the chest.

Even hit, the detective did not go down. He and his partner returned fire, striking Mad Dog.

Seeing her son shot down was more than Ms. Johnson could bear as she rushed without thinking toward her oldest child, probably saving the boy's life in the process. "Oh my lord! Oh my lord!" Ms. Johnson repeatedly screamed as she fell at her son's side pausing the officers from shooting.

Seeing their suspect down, the officers rushed over, pulling Ms. Johnson away from her son.

"Let me go!" Angry, she fought to be released.

As the crime scene was secured, other police officers had by now been dispatch to the 415 call of officer down. Ced disappeared over the backyard fence and was nowhere to be found. Some responding officers was combing the neighborhood to look for him. Even a house-to-house search produced nothing.

Meanwhile, Mad Dog was transferred to the Martin Luther King Jr. medical center where he was in surgery for thirteen hours to remove several slugs from the brief shoot-out. He was later transferred to the Los Angeles County Jail Hospital.

CHAPTER 36

Ced ran from yard to yard until he came to Wilmington Avenue and Alondra Boulevard. Then he proceeded to an apartment complex a block over. From there, a fellow gang associate drove him to his spot in Long Beach. He was never identified. However, Mad Dog was charged with murder and multiple attempted murders and was convicted. A few years into his sentence, he received a letter without a return address:

Greetings, Comrade,

I know this barua will find you standing firm under the circumstance. Over the past couple of years, your OBG has been moving in the shadow, but it's hard in this world without my (dog). I been trying to find the words to comfort you after those devils gave you all that time, but that shit stagnated. Yet with you gone, a nigga is holding it down for mom and the young soldier.

You know Kim had a little girl last year in June hood month, so not only is a Crip on his daddy thang, but you're a uncle. By the time you get this, you should have also received some bread.

Damn, cuz! Just trying to comprehend life without freedom leaves me at a loss for words, but being cut from the rag you cut from, I know strength is in your heart. My love and loyalty will forever

*stand firm for my day one six brother. When you
need me, holla at mom's. I got your back for life, and
that's on Nutty.*

From the cradle to the grave,
Six Time Solid

After reading the letter again, Mad Dog put it back in its enve-
lope, wiped the sweat off the bridge of his nose, and laid back.

Book Two

Wiccit Ways
Don't Sleep

CHAPTER 37

"May I help you, sir?"

I slid the note across the counter to the teller. She read it, looks up in shock, and read it again. I continue to calmly stand there with my head slightly down and my hands in my pocket. Looking at me again, then looking around caused me to do the same. Realizing no one was paying us any attention, the bank teller opened the cash drawer and began sliding stacks of bills to me, which I was stuffing in a briefcase I carried. From past experience, I know each stack held ten thousand dollars. Once the drawer was empty, I walked out the bank without a backward glance. Another day another dollar.

Once I reached my van, I drove around to the front of the bank and let the little boy out to join his mother inside. See, on the note was a picture of the boy tied up with a gun to his head that I'd taken earlier. Being big on detail, I never did a lick without extensive research. Therefore, I surveyed this particular bank for some weeks and learned the schedule of most of its employees. Learning this specific teller was a single mother, I put together a plan to work around that. Earlier today, I used the knowledge of his mother's name to convince the boy to ride with me. Promising I would take him to his mom sealed the deal. His picture on the note along with a few choice words guaranteed my financial come up. He was now with her. The rest is history.

CHAPTER 38

It's been over three years since Mad Dog and I had our confrontation with the pigs. He got lucky that day and escaped with his life. Because the murder in Watts was circumstantial, Mad Dog was never charged. However, the shoot-out is what cost him his freedom. "The life we live."

Since that situation, I did contemplate a safer acceptable lifestyle, but I got mouths to feed so I got back on the grind. After I left the bank, I ditched the van on Greenleaf Boulevard, leaving it in flames as I strolled to South Park to retrieve my car, which I left there earlier. I drove to the hood to find Lil Monsta or Little Crip Ced after stashing the briefcase in the trunk.

Since Mad Dog fell, Lil Ced has taken over the role of man of the house. Ms. Johnson was really down after losing Sissy and almost losing her firstborn as well. However, like most black women in the ghetto with children, she was proud, stubborn, and strong. Slowly, she began to bounce back. As I drove from street to street, collecting my thoughts, I see some homegirls. Since I can't spare the time, I honk the horn at keep and kept driving on. Not seeing Lil Ced or my brother, I decided to go home and put up this money. When I drove into my yard, I noticed my girl Kim was here.

"What's up, boo?" I greet her with a kiss and two hands full of ass.

"I decided to eat lunch at home today," she answered. What's up with you?"

I crashed on the couch, ignoring the question. I then grabbed the stereo remote and played Scarface on the CD changer. I take five

C-notes out the briefcase before putting the rest in the closet safe. Then I showered, got dressed, and fired up a blunt. When I returned to the living room, Kim was gone. So is two of the five notes I left on the couch, but it's all good. I'm out.

CHAPTER 39

Lil Monsta and Lil Crip Ced were also in traffic. They left school at lunch. To them, it was considered a full day. Now in his late teens, I gave cuz my Chevy. He and Lil Ced took full advantage of that. Both high school students and fully active in the hood, transportation was valuable. So as they were cruising around with music blasting, they were looking to see what the day would produce.

"Cuz," Lil Monsta spoke to his friend as they sat at a red light, "we need to go to the stadium and stack some ends." The stadium is the Grandee apartments in the hood. "Tonight, everybody bloccin to the Universal CityWalk for the Lil Boosie concert. You know it's gone be hella bitches."

Lil Ced gave a slight smile but said nothing. He was the silent type of nigga who rarely spoke. His actions was his speech. So Lil Monsta usually did the talking, knowing his friend was listening. As soon as they entered the stadium, Lil Ced saw a crackhead who owed him money. Pointing, he said, "Cuz, there go Windel!"

"That fool had better have my ends."

Monsta pulled up beside the crackhead. When he noticed who was in the car, he attempted to run. However, Lil Ced was already exiting the vehicle before it came to a complete stop.

"Come here, mothafucka!" Ced growled as he tripped Windel from behind.

The smoker fell hard. Rolling onto his back, eyes big as silver dollars, he stuttered, "C-C-Come on, man! I-I-I'm on my way n-now to pump gas for a few dollars."

"Shut up, fool!" Ced grabbed the crackhead by the pocket.

"What you got?"

By now, Monsta joined his partner. Together they emptied everything out his front and back pockets. In the end, all they found was a half-smoked cigarette, an empty lighter, and three cents. Seeing nothing of value, Lil Ced slugged Windel a couple times in the rib. Monsta kicked him in the ass to increase the humiliation.

"Next time I see you," Lil Ced warned, "you better have something for me."

Scrambling to his feet, the crackhead ran off before any more violence could come his way.

"Cuz, these smokers never learn!" Monsta laughed.

"Shit, we don't either," Lil Ced countered. "We keep giving credit."

They walked together to the apartment building in the back of the stadium. When they smelled the strong aroma of marijuana, they quickened their steps.

CHAPTER 40

Back in traffic, I stopped to check on Grandmom's before heading to the stadium. As I pulled into the complex, I noticed my little brother's car parked on the wrong side of the street, so I parked behind it. When I walked in the spot, I saw a couple of the young Nutties sitting around, drinking forties of Olde English and smoking. I nodded a "What's up?" as I went to the kitchen where I found Lil Ced at the small table, cutting crack up into rocks.

When he saw me approach, he smiled and stood where we exchanged the six boy hug (a half hug and six fist pounds). "What's up, big homie?" he greets me.

"What's up, my nigga!" I return the greeting. "I see you getting yo money."

"Yea, we going to the walk tonight so a nigga tryin' to get my dollars up. What's up with you, Crip?"

I leaned in, lowering my voice so only he could hear me. "I hit a lick earlier and got some work for you and lil bro when y'all get six minutes to holla." I answered. "Where's Monsta?"

"Cuz in the back, working the window." He added, remembering, "Oh yea, I got a letter from Mad Dog for you at mom's house."

"Supa," I said as I proceeded to the back to find my brother.

As soon as I walked in the room, I fell out laughing, seeing monsta sitting in a chair at the window, making a sale. The fat hoe next door was knelt between his legs, sucking his dick. When my little brother noticed me laughing by the door, he looked embarrassed as he pushed Bertha away and zipped up after drying himself on her shirt. I continued laughing as I approached cuz with a head nod.

68

"Nigga, ain't no hand shaking until you wash those things. All that gel, you need rubber gloves if you gone be running your fingers through that bitch's hair." This statement caused both brothers laughing.

With the disrespect, Big Bertha stormed from the room. "Fuck y'all niggas!" She spat, which only increased the laughter of the two brothers.

Spying another crackhead at the window, Monsta went to make the sell before rejoining his big homie and brother.

"Nigga, why yo ass ain't in school?" I asked with fake concern, hitting Monsta in the chest.

Quick to respond, Monsta countered with a blow to my chest that made me more proud than mad. I repeated what I'd just told Lil Crip Ced. My bro couldn't hide his excitement. "No shit, Crip. When?"

See, I'd used the two young Nutties before on licks, so I was completely confident in their push. "Just be ready when I bounce," I said. "I want y'all to ride with me somewhere."

"Shit, nigga, I'm ready now," he replied.

A couple hours later, after visiting in the stadium, we were on the I-110 headed toward Carson on the way to Harbor City. Getting off on Gaffey Avenue. I parked across the street from a small shopping center that had a jewelry store. I then explained the details of our lick. "I've been watching that store for over a week," I explained. Not interested in the product inside as much as the money pouch I observed the owner take to the bank to be deposited each Friday evening around five o'clock, the two young soldiers listened intently as I continued. "From the traffic I see coming and going, I think we can come upon some quick ends. It's all about timing."

We sat there a little while longer, just watching and discussing some strategy. On the way back, I let the homies know we'd be coming each day for the next week to continue getting them comfortable with the area. I dropped them off in the hood and bounced.

I recently started flippin' this freak who was a cheerleader for Gardena. A couple of times a week, I began picking her and a couple of her girls up after practice. I knew the type, car hops and gold diggers. Eventually, I'll probably end up flippin' them all. I smiled when I pulled up. I fire up the half a stick of lovely I had in the ashtray and leaned back. The whip got bitches jockin' for attention, but I won't fuck off a plan already in motion. I noticed the sexy Latina headed my way, trailed by two equally bad bitches. Falicia, a chocolate fat ass black girl with nonstop camel toe, and Isabla, another thick Mexican freak with lips made to suck dick. Every time she thought Maria was not looking, she made sure I could see her licking them, knowing what I was thinking. Since they all insisted on being in the front, I could admire each female close up. As we rode, they talked, laughed, and flirted. I was dropping them off one by one. As I drove away from Falicia's house, Maria snuggled even closer and started stroking my inner thigh. My dick got hard fast. She had a look that I recognized as a slut. I was glad we met. She sucked my dick better than Kim. As we cruised around, I knew it wouldn't be long before all her rubbing would lead to her mouth pleasuring me orally.

CHAPTER 41

It's Friday. Monsta, Lil Ced and I were once again parked across from magnificent jewelry store. Just like before, the Japanese owner closed the store and left carrying a deposit pouch. We followed him to the Bank of America and put the pouch into the night deposit box after entering a code and leaving. Every Friday for a month, we repeated the same routine until each detail was memorized. When it was time to execute, I let my young locs know it was time to put in work. "Today's the day, my niggas," I schooled. "We know dude makes his move no later than six o'clock. His script never changes, so ain't no need to follow him today. We gone set up ship at the Walmart next door. There's some phone booths out front."

I explained the plan. It was early. By 5:30 a.m., Monsta is at the booth, choppin' it up with whoever he was with on the phone, while I sat low in the back of the van behind the rear doors and Lil Ced was behind the wheel. Sure enough, right before six, the Jap was heading toward the drop box with pouch in hand. For some reason, that pouch looked supa fat today. Never even giving any interest to his immediate surroundings, the Jap never broke stride as I exited the van in all black, carrying a 12-gauge pump.

As I got closer, he finally felt my presence 'cause he turned to look back, missing Monsta who was approaching swiftly, carrying a bat. Before he could turn back, Monsta struck the Jap in the head. He was out before he hit the ground.

"Get the ends," I tell Monsta, while I went through his pockets to retrieve his keys.

As the victim regained consciousness, all he saw was the tail-lights of both his vehicle and the van retreating. We met up in the alley back in the hood where I searched his truck for anything of further value. Without any other valuables, we proceeded back to the stadium in the van. We entered the spot with the pouch and locked ourselves in a back room to tally up out lick. Empting the money on the bed, we counted it. Each came out a little over twelve Gs apiece.

"Cuz, that was the shift!" Lil Ced said joyfully, stacking his take by denomination. When is the next one?"

I smiled. "Patience, my nigga," I said and fired up the half blunt I still had from earlier.

CHAPTER 42

When I got home, Kim was washing dishes. I sat in the living room to read Dog's letter. Before I could finish, Little Nicki came running at me, happy with love. "Daddy, what you doing?" she asked in her tiny voice.

Trying to concentrate on what I was reading, I ignored her. Once I was finished, I grabbed her, tickling her and loving the light in her eyes as she giggled uncontrollably, making me laugh too. We played until Kim came and interrupted out fun. "Nichole, it's time for bed. Your ass gone be acting a fool in the morning when it's time to get up for school," she warned. Not wanting to leave me, she protested but eventually go about her business. I laughed, seeing her sassiness.

With Nicki tucked in, Kim and I watched some TV on the couch. Before long, I pulled her on my lap, and we were making out like back in the days. As I rubbed her breast and nibbled her neck, she asked half moaning if I was home for the night. "Yes," I responded, never interrupting my flow.

This put a big smile on my queen's face as she pulled me from the couch toward our room. Once there, Kim sat at the edge of the bed, unbuttoning my pants, while I removed my shirt. Once I stood naked in front of her, she began stroking my dick and licking all over the head like a fat chick with an ice cream cone, all the time moaning, "Ummm, baby!" while attacking my meat.

My knees were weakening as I admired her enthusiastic performance. "Damn, boo!" I let out a moan of my own. "You gone have a nigga nut all over your ass if you don't slow down," I whispered, listening to the sexy, hungry noises she made as her mouth continued its assault.

Looking up at me, Kim sucked my dick deep into her mouth, holding me there as I squirmed from the intense pleasure. She didn't intend for me to cum in her mouth, so when she felt my dick get iron hard and my body going stiff, she pulled back, running her tongue up and down the large throbbing vain under my dick before forcing me to sit down. Quickly stripping naked, I could see her pussy was freshly shaved, which made my mouth water. The fact that she wore no panties only added to the need.

Licking my lips, I said, "Oh yea, boo, that pussy look good!" She slowly rubbed her finger up and down the lips, wetting them and offering me a taste, which I happily licked clean while she climbed on top of me. We kissed passionately, sharing her juices until she kissed a trail down my body, stopping at my dick. Then she sucked on my balls lovingly one at a time. "Stop bullshitting, boo," I moaned while jerking all over the bed.

I tried bringing her pussy around toward my head, but she refused, once again taking my dick into her mouth so deep that all I could do was grab her head and fuck her mouth. Once again, she pulled back. This time, she turned her back to me, went on her knees, and laid her head in the mattress. Reaching back, Kim pulled her ass cheeks apart, revealing her pretty wet pussy, leaving no doubt that she wanted a nigga to hit the pussy from the back. My dick was leaking cum already, but as I climb behind her and grabbed a hand full of soft chocolate, I couldn't resist leaning forward and getting a taste of her asshole. This made her arch her back deeper and wiggle her hips, helping me get my tongue into her tight pink ass. When it's nice and wet inside and out, I slowly worked my thumb in her asshole while I gently lick up and down her pussy lips, blowing and gently sucking her clit as she orgasmed back to back. Needing to drink her sweet juice, I shove my tongue deep into her pussy, flicking back and forth to her clit. Unable to take much more, Kim fell flat on her stomach, trying to get away, but I had a lock on the pussy till she came again. Before she could recover, I put a pillow under her pelvis and slid my dick deep in one stroke, almost losing control myself. "Oh my god!" I moaned 'cause the pussy was warm and wet, gripping like a vice. Grasping her hips, I moved in and out and side to side, trying to touch every part of her pussy.

"Fuck this pussy, daddy!" Kim started talking shit. I hit without pause, fucking her through another orgasm. The pussy was so wet, I felt her juices all over my balls. Feeling my own nut rising, I pulled swiftly out her pussy and went balls deep in her asshole. This sends us both into a state of uncontrolled pleasure. Now without any remorse, I fucked Kim's asshole until I cum deep inside, collapsing on her back. Resting until my dick go soft, we drifted off to sleep extremely happy.

Barely able to get out of bed the next morning, I dragged myself to the shower. Kim and Nichole were already gone. From the pain in my back, though I was cool with that, I seriously doubt I could give a repeat performance so soon. After an extra hot shower and a good breakfast left in the microwave by Kim, I sat in front of the TV and dozed till the afternoon.

CHAPTER 43

In the hood, Monsta was up early on his way to school with pockets full of money. Lil Ced texted him early, also in a festive mood. "I'm gone drive myself today bro. I'll see you at the high."

After the Watts murders couldn't be charge to Mad Dog, Ms. Johnson was given back his Cadillac, which was in her name. Lil Ced immediately took possession of it as his means of transportation. Monsta stopped to wash his ride on Central Avenue and Compton Boulevard, believing that because of the early hour, he would be safe in enemy territory. However, while in the process of vacuuming, four young men around his age came up to the car and hit him up.

"What's up, blood?" One of them asked with attitude. "Where you from, blood? Monsta ignored him, continuing his business.

Another of the boys blocked his path as he was rounding the car. "Hey, blood! You hear the homie talking? Where you from, fool?" he questioned.

Unable to contain his anger, Monsta shoved the dude to the ground. hissing, "Nigga this, Nutty!" Before he could say another word, he was struck from behind. As he turned to retaliate, someone else hit him from the side. Monsta found himself fighting all four rivals, refusing to go down or run. "Nigga this, Crip!" Monsta was saying the whole time, going blow for blow.

Out of nowhere, he was struck above the ear with a bottle. Dazed, he fell as blood ran down the side of his face. Seeing the advantage, the four young boys increased their assault, punching and kicking Monsta, not willing to let him recover.

In the early morning drama, a female voice came out a yard. "Y'all stop that! Help, police!" she was screaming loudly at the group while running toward the boys. The four broke up and ran away. When she reached Monsta, she helped him to his feet and used the tile she was carrying when she left her house to slow the flow of blood from his head. "Lord, I tell you," she was saying, "stupid ass niggas always fuckin' with folks."

As she tended to his wound, Monsta began to notice she was not an old woman, by any means. She lived across from the car wash. She noticed him washing his car earlier. Hearing the commotion, she rushed from her home, not bothering or even paying attention to what she was wearing. Now Monsta was focusing more on her hard nipples and wide hips than his injuries, though he was glad she chose to rescue him. Her name was Shawnda. She tried to get Monsta to come to her house so she could treat his wounds, but he insisted he was okay.

"I'm good, ma," he was saying.

"Boy, you need to stop playin' though," she countered. "Your ass is bleedin'. You might even need stitches." She used a dish towel to slow the flood of blood.

"Naw, boo, I'm cool," Monsta assured her. "But thanks for your help and concern." He pulled out a roll of bills, offering her some money for her help.

Seeing all that money made her pause a little, but she declined his offer with a smile. "That's probably why those clowns was messing with you," she said. "That's just too much money to be carrying around. What's your name anyways?" Shawnda asked, giving Monsta the towel so he can hold it himself as he prepared to leave.

"Curtis," he answered.

She smiled. "You need to go get that cut fixed. That's my house,"—she pointed—"stop by so I know you made it."

As she returned to her yard, all Monsta could do was smile to himself as he watched her leave. "Damn!" he said to nobody. "With all that ass, she can be sure I'll come through."

As he drove off, his thoughts shifted to where those slobs went.

CHAPTER 44

By Christmas, Monsta, Lil Ced, and I had successfully robbed three more jewelry stores and a couple of drug spots. We all put money away and was looking forward to enjoying the holiday season, bringing in the New Year like true bosses. All over the city of Compton, people were in a festive mood. Making their own preparations this year, Kim intended to take Nichole up to meet her uncle Mad Dog for the first time. Though it was hard, he was able to get transferred closer to us. We believed it was time we gave him a nice Christmas too.

I also had one last lick before our little holiday fun. I made a deal to buy two bricks and laid down the script to my brother and Lil Ced as to my intentions. "Peep game, my niggas," I schooled. "We run this play for eight o'clock at the willow tree inn. Since I'm supposed to be alone, as is he, I'll need y'all to lay low until he and I make the transaction. When I give the signal (like butta), you two rush in and tie the clown up. I'll secure the product and scratch."

We bounced at seven fifteen. Minutes before showtime, we're in the room, watching BET. When I got the text that he arrived, I texted back the room number. Monsta and Lil Ced went to wait in the bathroom. When the knock came to the door, I answered it, checking the peephole first to make sure he was alone.

"What's up, player?" I greeted him when he entered.

I relock the door. Not one for procrastinating, I grabbed the duffle bag from under the bed and tossed it to the connect. "Check it," I said. "Thirty Gs a stack." After counting the stacks, he placed 'em back into the bag and reached for his cell. "Hold up, nigga.

What's up?" I asked, grabbing his wrist and my gun in one motion. "This shit is supposed to be between us. You tryin' to play me, fool?"

Seeing the danger in my eyes, he said, "Come on now, C. You know I don't get down scandalous." He shook his wrist free and continued the call. He spoke into the phone and hung up. I didn't consider him having backup, which was naive on my part, considering. But the deal was going down, there was no turning back. Plus, I had the locs in the bathroom. "I don't go walking around with two birds," he continued. "Relax, we good."

Monsta and Lil Ced could hear the whole exchange. They were focused on the mission.

When a second knock came, Ron went and peeped out. "That's my boy," he said, opening the door just enough for a hand to push a supermarket shopping bag through. "I'll be down in a minute," Ron told the owner of the hand as he took the bag and closed and relocked the door. "See what I mean, C. Just business, baby." Ron smiled, placing the bag next to the duffle.

Still on point, I watched as he took the product from the bag and extended one for my inspection. I pulled out my little buck knife and slit a small hole in the package. After rubbing some of the powder on my gums, I felt the expected numbing in my mouth. I watched the D-Boy as he started transferring the money from the duffle bag to the supermarket bag.

In a slightly raised voice, I announced, "Oh yea, player, *like butta.*"

Like a scene from the *Unusual Suspect*, Monsta and Lil Ced busted out the bathroom, guns drawn. Shocked, Ron jumped back, dropping the money.

"What the fuck is this, C?" he asked me.

Before I could respond, Lil Ced slapped him across the mouth with his pistol. "Shut up, punk!" Lil Ced growled. "If you wona live, do what you're told."

The D-Boy had no choice but to cooperate and was even more shaken when Monsta began to put handcuffs on him. Come on, man! All this ain't called for."

In response, Lil Ced hit him again, dislodging his front tooth and leaving him whimpering like a baby. After his hands and ankles were tied up. They gagged him and put in the bathtub naked. During all this, I loaded both money and product in the duffle bag.

"Y'all ready to bounce, cuz," I told the young Nutties.

"What about the other clown?" Monsta asked. "Won't he see us leaving?"

"Don't trip, Crip. We going down the back stairs."

CHAPTER 45

Unbeknownst to us though, the D-Boy's partner was on his way back to the room. Sitting in the car, he started wondering what was taking Ron so long. He was on his way to investigate. As we left the room, we came face-to-face with a dude. We didn't know until the guy asked, "Where's Ron?" Noticing our hesitation, he was reaching toward his waist.

I also went for my weapon, but the guy made the move first. He started firing. Diving for cover, Monsta and Lil Ced hit the floor, but not before a bullet struck Monsta in the shoulder. My bullet hit the guy a second later. He fell but was still firing off rounds. His weapon, however, was dislodged from his hand when he hit the concrete ground. In a flash Lil Ced retrieved the gun and shot the stranger in the face and head before I managed to get him and Monsta back in the room. The motel guest, concerned from the sound of gunfire, came to look.

"What now, big homie?" Lil Ced questioned me in a stressed tone.

Attending to my little brother's wound, I ignored him but thinking of the same shit. Once Monsta's bleeding slowed down, I ordered him to hold a wet rag over the flesh wound, "Hold that, bro." I then told Lil Ced we'd be leaving through the fire escape. I had Lil Ced get my brother to the window and ready to go while I went to the bathroom where we left Ron.

"Well, my nigga," I informed him, "looks like you ain't gonna survive after all." I put two bullets in his forehead.

I went back the room to see the locs ready to bounce. I checked the room, wiping down everything we could have touched. I put the bloody rags from Monsta in the duffle with the money and climbed out the window. We made our way down the fire escape to the alley. When we reached the street, a police car was already in the lot. I told the homies to wait across the street by the bus stop and I would get the van. Knowing it was only a matter of time before more police arrived, I gave them the duffle and ran to our ride. Leaving from the alley again, I scooped up the young Nutties and headed back to the city.

Once we were a sufficient distance away from the motel, I looked back at my brother. "You okay, loc?"

"I will be once we're back in the hood."

I jumped on the 91 freeway straight to the stadium.

CHAPTER 46

The next morning, Monsta woke up a little stiff. It had been difficult getting comfortable with his injury. When we reached the stadium last night, one of the homegirls cleaned his wound, poured some peroxide on it, and bandaged him up. Looking around, he could see me and Lil Ced still sleep. Before long, he dozed again.

CHAPTER 47

Since meeting Shawnda, Monsta and her shared company a few times. He got to know her better and even met and liked her three-year-old son. Still recovering from the flesh wound, he decided to visit. A little after ten o'clock, he knocked a few times until he heard soft footsteps approaching the door. Peeking out the curtain, Shawnda smiled upon seeing Monsta. However, the smile disappeared when she noticed he was hurt.

"What happened to you, Curtis?" she asked as soon as she opened the door.

Monsta gave her a quick kiss as he entered and went to sit on the couch without a response. Shawn came over to sit beside him.

"Bae, what happened?" she asked again, concerned.

"Just a little scratch." He shrugged it off.

Since he began coming, she started keeping a couple of beers in the refrigerator. Wanting him to relax, she got up to get one without his asking. He couldn't help but admire the way her ass muscles flexed when she walked. "Are you hungry?" she yelled from the kitchen. "I still have some chicken left from dinner."

"That's cool," he responded.

After he ate, they cuddled and watched a movie on Netflix. By the end of the movie, the food was long forgotten. The cuddling turned into full groping till she pulled away, disappearing into her room. She returned wearing a long T-shirt and carrying her cowboy blanket. When she sat next to Monsta, he discovered the T-shirt was all she had on, allowing him complete access to her ample warm flesh. Shawn noticed he was having a difficult time with his sore shoulder.

AGAINST ALL ODDS

"Let me help you with that," she whispered in his ear. She proceeded to remove his shoes, socks, and pants. When he was naked, she saw how hard his dick was and gave it a good squeeze. "Ummm, bae!" she purred kissing, the head and licking off the leaking pre-cum. Monsta just closed his eyes and leaned back, enjoying the magic Shawnda preformed with her soft lips and tongue. While she sucked his dick, she made loud smacking and humming noises. "Ummm, ummm! Slurrrp!"

He was unable to sit still. Monsta's ass was dancing all over his seat as he prepared to fill her mouth with his cum, but she needed him in her wet pussy. With a final deep throat trick, she held his dick deep in her mouth, twisting her head from left to right, massaging her tonsils with the head of his dick. Then without warning, she raised up and as he slipped out her mouth, his fat member slapped against his stomach. "Hey, boo!" His eyes flew opened in disappointment. Without saying anything, she stood up, took off her shirt, and straddled his lap. Putting a nipple in his mouth to shut him up, she then grabbed his hard dick at the lips of her wet pussy. With one good arm, Monsta pulled her ass cheeks apart and drove himself halfway into her. "Damn, baby!" He moaned as her tight warmth accepted him. "That feels so hot," he continued as he drove balls deep on his next lunge.

"Oh my god!" Shawnda began crying as she orgasmed. "That's it, bae," she said as she bounced her pussy up and down his dick, rubbing her clit for another orgasm. Without losing him inside her, she turned around with her feet on the outside of Monstas thighs. With her hands on his knees, she was riding the dick like an obsessed horse jockey riding toward the finish line.

For quite some time, the living room was filled with the sound of sex. Monsta couldn't pull his eyes away from her pussy sliding up and around his dick over and over as her ass slapped against his pelvic muscle. Finally, unable to hold out any longer, Monsta began thrusting up with Shawnda's every lunge until his cum shot deep up her pussy and she soaked him with sweet juice.

Unable to move soon after, they sat with her back to his chest and his dick still locked in her pussy till he was too soft to stay in.

85

CHAPTER 48

The Christmas and New Year celebrations went down without any drama. We partied like real niggas should. By mid-January, shit began to settle. Mad Dog met a female on POF and was feeling good about the future. Monsta was low-key on Shawnda's head game and was spending even more time with her and her son. He and Lil Crip Ced were still serving dope in the stadium and pushing like young Nutties were raised too.

With Mad Dog almost gettin' the gas chamber and Sissy getting murdered, Ms. Johnson was never able to get back to her former self. She retired to spend her time at home or church a sad resemblance to the lonely cat down the block.

All the jewelry store robberies received attention in the news, so I'd been laying low, working for parks and recreation while Kim and I planned a small wedding on my birthday at the end of the month.

CHAPTER 49

O n the day I was to be married, shit seemed unreal to me. I woke up to an empty house since Kim and Little Nicky spent the night at her mom's spot on some tradition type shit. I fired up a blunt of that white willow and put my thoughts in perspective. I called my little brother and best man, already knowing cuz was still hung over from the bachelor's party last night. "What's up, nigga?" I spoke when he finally answered. "Get your ass up, fool. We got some real shit going down today."

Hearing my voice, he sat up on his elbow. "Okay, bro, just stop yelling. My head's about to blow up!"

"Yea well, my head's about to explode too, but it's from this blunt I just blew!" I laughed at my own joke. "Get that ass up, my nigga. I'll be over to scoop you up in a hour. We can get you some coffee and breakfast before we get dressed."

"Is Big Momma rollin' with us?" He wanted to know.

"Naw, bro. She with Kim. Them doing their girl thing. They probably took her to some Chippendales bullshit so she can get her old school grove on." The thought of that had us both laughing hard as I hung up.

*****

Kim was also up early. Nichole hated getting her hair combed so she wanted to get an early start. When she entered the kitchen, it was already busy with activity. The smell of food and fresh coffee wiped all the sleep out of her system. The biggest surprise though was the sight of her daughter sitting quiet while her granny did her hair. Big Momma was at the stove, ordering everyone around as always.

"Girl, you sit on down and eat something fo' it gets too late," she ordered. "You know it ain't gone be another chance till the reception," she added, setting a plate of eggs and bacon in front of her. Kim just smiled at her daughter. "We been in here chillin' as you young folks say." Big Momma never stopped talking.

"Mommy, Gran-Gran said I get to help you and Daddy cut the cake," Nicki said excitedly:

"Yes, baby, that's true," Kim replied.

The remainder of the morning was full of activity in the house as the women got dressed and enjoyed their lady talk. By the time the limo arrived, the three women and little girl was more than ready to get to the church.

CHAPTER 50

Over at Watts, the others were getting ready for the wedding too, but for very different reasons. Some associates of Big Vine had seen the announcement of the wedding on Facebook and took this as their opportunity to avenge their comrade's death.

"Yea, man. I told you this nigga Ced was roll dog with the fool whose sister we smoked."

"Yea, I did hear her brother beat Vine's murder on a technicality but got washed on a shoot-out with the pigs."

"Whatever, my boy," Sweet Pea said with a distant look in his eyes. Today we get some get back."

"Hell yea!" Lil Cee cheered. "Let's do this."

CHAPTER 51

The ceremony was beautiful. Kim looked sexy and glamorous, and I was fly crippin' as always. We both smiled like fools in love when the pastor said, "You may kiss the bride." Kim's mother and Big Momma both sat on the front pew, crying as we proceeded out the church where our close family and friends waited, ready to shower us with rice.

CHAPTER 52

L il Crip Ced noticed the gray Chevy Nova parked across the street from the church. At first, he thought it was a guest waiting for the ceremony to start. Big Ced and Kim did know a lot of people. Still, the occupants in the car looked out of place for some reason, so Lil Ced got his Glock 40 just to be safe.

With Ced and Monsta participating in the wedding, he didn't get to reveal his thoughts, but he posted up just inside the church entrance and watched the ceremony from there. As the people gathered outside the door, waiting for the bride and groom to exit, Lil Ced noticed how the dudes in the Chevy seemed tense as their focus locked in at the front of the church.

CHAPTER 53

When the people began gathering around outside, Lil Cee and Sweet Pea sat up, watching the church door more intensely.

Making sure his gun had one in the chamber, Sweet Pea broke the silence. "Well, bro, it looks like it's our time to shine." As he was making this statement, the photographer was just backing out the church ahead of the couple to capture their exit on film. "It's on!" Sweet Pea said as he swung the passenger door open. With gun in hand, he rounded the front of the car.

Simultaneously, Lil Cee came from behind the wheel, also armed. Both killers never hesitated as they crossed the street. The guests were watching the couple's exit so no one noticed the two killers approaching, except Lil Ced. He also made his move.

CHAPTER 54

Lil Ced saw the two men get out their car with guns and imme-diately advanced in that direction. However, Ced and Kim were already standing outside on the steps, smiling when the gunfire began.

"Get down! Get down!" Lil Ced was yelling, firing his own weapon as he ran toward the two dudes trying to assassinate his OBG.

In the hail of bullets, people were running and screaming, duck-ing and falling.

Out of reflex, I pushed Kim to the ground. Before I could get down myself, I was hit multiple times in the upper torso. I fell at Kim's feet unable to do anything but stare at the sky. A few of those slow to respond were also gunned down as bullets rained on the cel-ebration, not rice.

Lil Ced ducked behind the bride and groom's limo to avoid being shot himself. However, his return gunfire succeeded in pre-venting the two gunmen from advancing further. When he managed to strike one, blowing half of his face away, the other clown ran, leav-ing behind the Nova and dead bodies behind as he vanished around the corner. Turning back to view the chaos, it was like a scene from a Hollywood movie. Seeing his big homie laid out, he rushed up the stairs where Kim was hysterically crying. As he knelt at their side, he knew, without a doubt, it was too late.

CHAPTER 55

Leading up to the funeral, Kim was in an extreme state of depression. Little Nichole had been staying with Big Momma 'cause Kim's condition prevented her from caring for her daughter's basic needs. She refused to go to work or answer the phone. Barely capable of going to the toilet, she was deteriorating by the day. However, as she woke up knowing that despite the pain, she had to get her ass up this morning and pull her shit together so she could go represent the love of her life. As she lay there thinking about the husband she lost, shame began to replace the feeling of depression because she knew she was disrespecting both the welfare of her daughter as well as the legacy of her man by exhibiting weakness.

Understanding she had to get her shit together, Kim wiped the last tear from her eyes and stepped out of the bed determined to live up to the expectations and confidence her friend, love, and king had in her. Going in the bathroom, she could not ignore what the mirror revealed. "Girl, you a mess!" she told herself.

While she went about the process of restoring her life back to a sense normal, she couldn't help but reflect on the life she'd lost and put some perspective to the life ahead. Now dressed, focused, and ready to reenter the game of life, Kim paused before leaving the apartment to ask God for the strength to endure.

"Mommy, Mommy!" Little Nichole ran at full speed toward her mother upon seeing her enter the funeral home.

It had been over a week since they were together. Fresh tears came to Kim eyes as she embraced her daughter. She also felt a renewed degree of shame, knowing she left her baby alone during her own grief. As the funeral came and went, mother and daughter never left each other's side. From that day forward, Kim was committed to honoring the man who owned her heart.

CHAPTER 56

Regardless of how hard Kim tried to rebound, life as a single mother was taking its toll. She'd gotten a second job but struggled to maintain a comfortable existence for her and her daughter.

"Girl, you better come get some of this easy money," her friend Ashley said as they talked on the phone.

Working the graveyard shift at the twenty-four-hour gas station was boring. Customers were few, but the late-night creeps never stopped. Plus, Kim missed the time she and Nichole spent together. As usual, Kim was passing the long hours on Facebook and gossiping with her BFF Ashley.

Since Ash was a stripper, she was making plenty of paper and had been consistently trying to convince Kim to join the ranks of exotic dancers. "Bitch," Ash added, "all that work you doing for those crumbs ain't the business. The streets are full of tricks, pretenders, and lonely ass niggas willing to give a boss bitch their paper. Shit, the pleasure I get from watching those niggas pay for the hopes of getting this good pussy is almost better than sex."

"Whatever, hoe," Kim said. "I'm still deciding."

Every day she was fighting to stay in her lane, but every night she was being pulled closer to the pole. After falling behind on some bills a couple months later, she called Monsta to see what he thought about her stripping. Not that she had to have his approval or anything like that, but Kim was still very much in love with Ced and did not want to disrespect her deceased husband's name.

Monsta heard the phone and wondered who could be calling him this late. Seeing the number, he sat up. "Hello," he answered, his heart beating double time.

"Hey, bro," Kim said.

"What's wrong, K?"

She smiled, hearing the stress in his voice. Since Ced's death, Monsta had been there for her and his niece, sometimes being overprotective. She could tell he was worried now, probably because of the late call. "Boy, ain't nothing wrong. I'm at work and wanted to talk to you."

Still believing something was wrong, Monsta was now wide awake and sitting at the side of the bed. "So what's up, K?" he asked again. "How's lil bit?"

"She cool. Big Momma keeps her every night I have to work. Yea, I gotta fall through and check on them both, Ced said. Nigga been chasin' this paper and neglecting my real people."

"What, you need some chips?"

Kim hesitated before answering, "No, at least not in the way you think. However, I would like to get your input on a move I'm about to make."

"Okay, holla."

Kim gave a small chuckle at how direct Monsta always was, just like his brother was. "Well, the hours I'm working is wearing me down," Kim admitted. "I'm changing it up. I'm about to start dancing."

For a minute, Monsta was lost. Then it dawned on him that she was talking about the strip club. Kim was quiet, waiting on his response and when he said, "Shit, sis, if that's what you wona do, you know I got your back." Monsta had always been supportive. To have his blessing meant a lot to her. "Don't be bringin' no niggas around my niece though," Monsta added, interrupting her thought.

She heard him giggle though so she knew he was saying some real shit. "Boy, you ain't my daddy," she countered, giggling herself.

Monsta knew his brother's death hit Kim hard and understood as well as respected the fact that she wanted to start living again. They talked a little while longer. After the conversation ended, Kim was a lot more confident in her decision to start dancing.

CHAPTER 57

Kim had been working at the body shop for a few months now. She was enjoying all the free time she and Nichole was spending together, taking and picking her up from school and outings on the weekends. Plus, she was now able to live a lifestyle she'd been accustomed to with Ced. She was often amazed at how niggas tricked off their money for pussy they never got. This was on her mind tonight when she walked into work, seeing all the dancers with G-strings full of money.

Once in her outfit as the sexy nurse, stethoscope and all, Kim hit the main floor to greet the clientele and network before her set on the main stage. She knew she was bad with ass and titties, capable of getting a nigga hard in her street clothes. Shit, she got Ced's attention. In her barely-there nurse's gear, she was a favorite in the club. Once she hit center stage and began sliding that pole between her ass cheeks, niggas start throwing paychecks, alimony, and child support payments at her feet to keep those ass cheeks poppin'.

While still making her rounds, Kim was stopped by one of the club's regular customers and offered a drink. While sitting in a booth, talking and sipping, she overheard some dudes in the next booth over mention Ced's name. This caused her to focus on their conversation. Although obviously quite drunk and talking in slurred speech, she could hear the dude in the Vikings football jersey bragging about a wedding he shot up. He was celebrating his homie's birthday, which was killed on the mission.

"Yea, cuz, at least we smoke that bitch ass nigga Ced before my boy Lil Cee fell from return fire. Man, I miss my dog," the man was saying.

Tears filled Kim eyes. She ran to the back, unable to listen further. While she sat on a chair in the dressing room, Kim was forced to relive the most painful day of her life. Knowing she had to do something, she got her cell from her locker and called Monsta.

Seeing the number on his phone, Monsta answered. Speak on it, sis. He and Lil Crip Ced was cut in traffic, checking traps. Kim was talking so fast, he couldn't fully understand what she was saying. "Slow down, sis. Slow down," he tried calming her down. However, he was only getting pieces of what she was saying. "Kim!" Monsta finally yelled into the phone, which cause her to pause and allow him to get what she was saying. "I'm on my way."

CHAPTER 58

She knew she couldn't allow this group to leave, so she put her emotions in check and freshened up before going back on the club's main floor to locate her husband's killer. It was not too difficult. All she had to do is follow the noise. The liquor was flowing still, and the four men in the booth were acting like fools. *Well, good,* Kim thought as she played the background and waited for the troops to come through.

As Kim was keeping her eyes on the group, her time on stage came. When the lights dimmed, the DJ announced, "And now, feature performer, every hustler's dream and every thug's ride-or-die chick, the sexiest nurse on the West Coast, Honeeey Diiip!"

To the heart-thumping beat and detailing lyrics of Lil Boosie's "Independent," Kim hit the stage like a hurricane, blowing the other dancers out the water with her amazing body and moves. With a name like Honey Dip and ass for days, she had both niggas and bitches lusting. Tonight, like every other, she was the center of attention. When she let the pole slide between her checks and started clapping her ass around it, customers were falling over each other to make it rain for her. She even noticed the clowns from table five was caught up in the moment, which was a good thing 'cause Monsta and Lil Ced arrived. From the look on their faces, pussy was the last thing on their minds.

Kim kept the crowd's attention through two more songs, ending her performance dry fucking the stage to Usher's "Confessions." In the end, Kim stood ankle deep in money of every denomination and exited while the stagehand collected the paper. Once she freshened up and got dressed, Kim made sure her money was locked away. Then she joined Monsta and Lil Ced at a corner table.

"Damn, K! After witnessing that, I'm at a loss for words," Monsta teased. This was his first time seeing her strip, and the erection he got watching his deceased brother's wife had him blushing.

"Boy, you crazy!" Kim giggled.

"Shit, if those clowns didn't take my brother's life, I'm sure all that ass would have," he continued. "But speaking on bro, can you run that down to me again that you heard."

Kim gave them a recap of the conversation she overheard form the men. When she was finished, they had no doubt these dudes were involved in Ced's death. Because of the dim lighting, Lil Ced couldn't make out the guys' faces, but that was irrelevant. The decision was made. With closing time fast approaching, Monsta and Lil Ced went outside to wait.

CHAPTER 59

Without a care in the world, the group of men continued to celebrate.

Sweet Pea was enjoying a lap dance, already warned about inappropriate contact with the dancers. "Bitch, I want some of this ass!" he told the young lady, grabbing her ass cheeks with two hands. Having had enough, the dancer tried to leave, only to be roughly pulled back. "Bitch, where you going?"

"Nigga, if you don't let me go, I'm gone kick your drunk ass," she was saying while struggling to get free.

The other men in the booth were enjoying the drama, laughing and cheering on Sweet Pea.

The ruckus again drew the attention of security, and they rushed over to end the drama.

"Fool, get your hands off me!" Sweet Pea was yelling as the huge guard snatched him up and escorted him and his crew to the door.

The group talked shit the whole way. Without weapons, they were no match for security. Outside, the men continued to curse as they staggered to their car, unaware that karma was about to strike with a vengeance.

CHAPTER 60

Lil Ced was the first to see the men being thrown out the club. "It's showtime, my nigga," he said, pointing.

He and Monsta retrieved their weapons from the stash and was more than ready. Seeing the fool responsible for taking his brother and homie's life caused a tear up, blurring his vision. He quickly wiped it away as he grabbed the AK-47 off the backseat.

The group of men crossed the parking lot in a festive mood. It was not until Lil Ced stepped from between two cars that they became aware the danger. Coming from the side, Monsta stepped into view. With only the hood call, "Ooowhup!" he pulled the trigger, and the automatic weapon spit death. With Lil Ced in front, unleashing his own deadly assault, the group didn't even get to blink before the life was blown from their bodies.

As quickly as it began, it was over. The infamous white Cadillac sped from the lot with only bodies and bullet shells left behind.

ABOUT THE AUTHOR

Cedric Westbrook was born in Fort Worth, Texas, but bred and raised in Compton, California.